MW01268662

THE HEALING TOUCH

Keeping the
Doctor-Patient Relationship
Alive Under Managed Care

David L. Cram, M.D.

Addicus Books, Inc.
Omaha, Nebraska

ADDICUS BOOKS

An Addicus Nonfiction Book

ISBN 1-886039-31-3

Cover design by George Foster.

Typography by Linda Dageforde.

The author gratefully acknowledges permission from the Mayo Foundation to use material from *Aphorisms* (Charles and William Mayo), collected by Frederick A. Willius. The Mayo Foundation for Medical Education and Research, 1997. All rights reserved.

Library of Congress Cataloging-in-Publication Data

Cram, David L. (David Lee), 1934-
     The Healing touch : keeping the doctor-patient
       relationship alive under managed care / by David L. Cram.
                    p.   cm.
     Includes bibliographical references.
     ISBN   1-886039-31-3 (al. paper)
     1. Physician and patient. 2. Managed care plans (Medical
care)—Psychological aspects.   I. Title.
       [DNLM: 1. Physician-Patient Relations. 2. Managed Care Pro-
grams—United States. W 62 C889h 1997]
R727.3.C73   1997
610.69'6—dc21
DNLM/DLC
For Library of Congress   97-17574
                                                                       CIP

Addicus Books, Inc.
P.O. Box 45327
Omaha, Nebraska 68145
Web site: http://members.aol.com/addicusbks

Printed in the United States of America
10 9 8 7 6 5 4 3 2 1

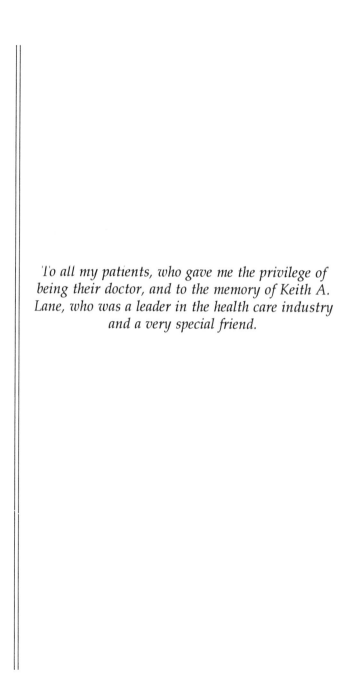

To all my patients, who gave me the privilege of being their doctor, and to the memory of Keith A. Lane, who was a leader in the health care industry and a very special friend.

Contents

Foreword

At a time when rapidly changing health care environments pose many threats to traditional doctor-patient relationships, master clinician Dr. David Cram has stopped to consider the fundamental relationships in good patient care. In this timely book, Dr. Cram examines the challenges that every health care professional faces in preserving the magical element of the doctor-patient relationship: the healing touch.

During an era when sophisticated biotechnology is worshipped at the expense of interpersonal skills, it is refreshing to read a book that reflects old-fashioned views on how to maintain a healthy doctor-patient relationship. *The Healing Touch* should be required reading for all medical professionals and should be a standard against which the humanity of health care reform is measured.

Dr. Cram has been recognized nationally as an outstanding physician and professor of dermatology, with many years dedicated to patients suffering from chronic and overwhelming skin diseases. From this experience he brings us clear and understandable portraits of the caring relationships that must exist between doctors and patients. Throughout his work, Dr. Cram reminds us all to recognize and exercise our power to shape the future of health care for the benefit of our patients.

Pamela A. Baj, DNSc, RN, FAAN
Professor of Nursing
San Francisco State University

Acknowledgments

I wish to thank the reviewers of my early manuscript—Marian Nelson, Daniel Kammer, Bruce Wintroub, and Julius Krevans—all of whom offered suggestions and kind remarks that spurred me to complete this book. I especially wish to acknowledge Pamela Baj. She, along with her husband Rick Glogau, offered invaluable ideas and support for *The Healing Touch*. Finally, I wish to thank my publisher, Rod Colvin of Addicus Books, and my editor Susan Adams. Both made the revising and completing of this work a pleasant and educational experience.

Acknowledgments

I wish to thank ... ...

Introduction

All of us harbor a basic need for interpersonal contact. At no time is this need greater than when we become ill. Although religious faith can be helpful, when disease strikes we almost always turn to our doctors for their knowledge and care. If the disease proves serious or chronic, we feel an even greater need for that special supportive touch from another human being who can give us hope or help lead us down the path to recovery. Doctors and other health care providers can provide that special touch that helps us heal.

When I retired from my private practice of dermatology, I began to reflect on the changes that the introduction of managed care has brought to our health care system and on the impact these changes are having on both doctors and patients. During the last few years of my practice, I noted that many new controls and restrictions were taking away some of the freedoms of practice I had enjoyed in the past. Many patients first had to be screened by a primary care physician who acted as a gate-keeper in deciding whether I, as a skin care specialist, could treat them. Although I had one of the most successful practices in my specialty, my patient volume was gradually reduced by market forces. Despite these changes, I never lost my love for the practice of medicine.

Our society is also demanding health care at lower costs. Patients are often receiving more selective and restrictive care to maintain these lower costs. Many states are experimenting with rationing health care, and the concept of managed care is becoming universal. Established health maintenance organizations (HMOs) are expanding and merging with other plans to accommodate more patients and to increase profits. More and more, doctors are seeking the salaried positions offered by these plans.

For many of today's private practice physicians, these changes are frightening. Doctors see their established practices shrink and their livelihoods threatened. There is no stopping this juggernaut, as the entire medical profession—including nurses, pharmacists, and dentists—must conform to the social and financial demands of the new system.

As I contemplated these changes, I became convinced that the loss of incentives under managed care might force more medical care providers to offer less of a healing touch to their patients. After delving more deeply into the literature on the subject, I found my concerns were justified. A study by the New England Medical Center of Boston concludes the physician-patient relationship has an important influence on a patient's health outcome and must be taken into account in light of current changes in the health care delivery system that may place this relationship at risk (Kaplan 1989).

Further, I have interviewed a number of patients to hear firsthand stories of their physicians' bedside manner (see chapter 7). Many report an insidious change in this aspect of patient care, which I and many other doctors feel is essential to the healing process (Kass 1992; Siegler 1993). During three decades of practice, I witnessed firsthand the rewards of a good bedside manner and observed that it could add to healing in a way that all the medications in the world could not match. I fear this crucial aspect of patient care could be lost in the ongoing health care revolution. I often refer to *bedside manner* and the *doctor-patient relationship* collectively as *the healing touch*. Hence the title of this book. I feel it expresses, in an even more compassionate way,

how a caring physician can have a profound re-
medial effect on a patient's disease and suffering.

I hope this book might serve as a resource
for health care professionals facing the challenges of preserving the healing touch in an environment of "hurry-up medicine" and "patient
quotas." Yes, we need to recognize a whole new
set of rules under managed care and learn to accept the fact that health insurance benefits are
more restrictive. But, we as physicians must
never lose sight of the fact that our primary concern is the welfare of our patients and the quality
of medicine we practice. A significant part of that
quality is the healing touch and the rewards it
brings into the lives of those entrusted to our
care.

A good physician makes the support of dignity an important part of his professional task, offering hope without deception, behaving seriously without solemnity, giving advice while respecting freedom. In so doing he tacitly recognizes and indeed demonstrates that he, like his patients, like any human being, is a being mysteriously in-between and yet pointed upward.

Leon R. Kass, MD
University of Chicago

The citizen doctor treats disease by going into things thoroughly from the beginning in a scientific way and takes the patient and his family into confidence. Thus he learns something from the sufferers. He does not give prescriptions until he has won the patient's support and when he has done so he aims at producing complete restoration to health by persuading the sufferer into compliance.

Plato

1

The Influence of Bedside Manner

The concept of bedside manner dates back 2,500 years, when Plato wrote the earliest known description of the doctor-patient relationship in *The Laws*. Plato writes that the best clinical medicine is practiced when the doctor and the patient have concluded a fully human relationship in which the technical aspects of care are placed in the human context (Siegler 1993). However, throughout much of history, doctors would not always fully inform patients of their conditions. This "code of silence" still exists today in some cultures. For example, a physician might not inform a cancer patient of his or her condition, believing that not knowing will enhance the patient's immunity, decrease anxiety and therefore extend life.

Fortunately, in the United States today, medical professionals recognize patients' need to know and understand their conditions. We realize that, especially with a serious or chronic disease, patients are vulnerable. What doctors say and how they act toward these patients can have a major effect on both the patients and their diseases. The will to get better and to remain upbeat irrespective of the illness can be a direct result of a sympathetic physician playing a significant role in the patient's life. S.H. Kaplan (1989) states, "The physician-patient relationship is a primary bond that may act as a social support to influence the patient's health status."

Good physicians realize that patients expect answers from their doctors. The manner in which a physician talks to the patient can affect the long-range outlook of the disease. Incorrectly done, it can result in such undesirable effects as noncompliance with therapy, more complicated testing, the need for higher doses of medication, more frequent office visits, longer hospital stays, or an increase in medical lawsuits. The patient may also decide to seek another doctor. If the goal of our society is to achieve better health care at reduced costs, a good bedside manner from health care providers obviously will play a significant role in reducing these costs.

Qualities of a good doctor

I believe the following are the qualities of a good doctor and the foundation of a good bedside manner:

- Intelligence
- Altruism
- Honesty
- Inquisitive mind
- Sense of humor
- Empathy

- Self-confidence
- Patience
- Sincerity
- Good memory
- Compassion
- Genuine concern for the welfare of others

How is bedside manner best applied?

To have medical knowledge and skill alone is not enough. To be truly effective in treating the sick, doctors and nurses must have good communication skills. In one sense, they are educators. Education helps patients make decisions. Doctors should allow patients to make shared decisions and be willing to walk the road to recovery with them (Herman 1985).

Many times when I was treating a patient with a difficult problem, I asked myself: "If this were a member of my own family, what would I do?" I wanted every patient to have the best care available. These thoughts often helped guide my decisions. When treating a chronic, recalcitrant skin disease like psoriasis, I knew I could not cure the disease since there is no cure. But I was confident that I could relieve the discomfort and often free the patient from significant disease for long periods of time. I believe the keys to my success were good communication, empathy, sharing decisions about therapy with the patient, and, perhaps most importantly, believing in my abilities and offering the patient encouragement every step of the way. I found that successfully treating this difficult skin disease was a challenge that brought me great satisfaction.

Evidence shows that encouraging patients to take an active role in their care can enhance therapeutic outcomes (Speedling 1985). Decisions concerning therapy should, whenever possible, attempt to incorporate the patient's preferences. This may not be possible in emergency situations, for patients with high dependency needs, or when the patient's psychological state clouds his or her judgment. In these situations, discussions with family members become very important in helping the physician decide how best to proceed with treatment.

Why do some doctors neglect bedside manner?

Some doctors regard a good bedside manner as simply irrelevant to the practice of medicine. It is not surprising that this attitude exists since interpersonal skills receive only token attention in the curricula of many of our medical schools. Studies indicate that interpersonal skills may even decline as medical education progresses (Helfer 1990).

Some new doctors, after years of exposure to illness and dying, become numb and indifferent as a means of self-protection. Unfortunately, such self-protective measures may render them unable to empathize. As these doctors either mask their feelings or deny them, they often regard patients as diseased bodies to be treated or as teaching case studies.

An American Medical Association survey conducted in 1993 reveals that public esteem for physicians has diminished during the last decade. The survey further shows that fewer than a third of patients think doctors spend enough time with them. Forty-four percent agree that "doctors act like they are better than other people" (*American Medical News* 1993). To many physicians these statistics may be troubling, but they may be the direct result of negative behavior, interpreted by patients as a lack of concern and caring. A positive outcome depends on behavior that is facilitating rather than dominating (Stewart 1984).

One meets with many men who have been fine students, and have stood high in their classes, who have great knowledge of medicine but very little wisdom in application. They have mastered the science, and have failed in the understanding of the human being.

William J. Mayo, M.D.

2

Learning Bedside Manner

Webster's dictionary defines *bedside manner* as "the attitude, approach and deportment of a doctor toward patients" (Webster 1992). However, it is much more complex. Bedside manner is actually a special skill that must be learned, practiced, and never taken for granted. There are few formal lectures given directly on the subject in many of our medical schools. Some doctors fail to properly apply it, and some even scoff at its importance.

The importance of role models

My experience has been that in the absence of formal lectures, a good bedside manner can be learned in two ways. The first is by *observation*—watching clinical instructors in medical training talk with patients and noticing their reactions. The second is by *reflec-*

tion—referring to one's own life experiences. By observing the interplay of words between the instructor and the patient, the alert medical student soon comes to recognize what effect certain words and demeanor have on patients. Hopefully the exchange will be a positive one. Unfortunately, if the instructor's pattern of communication with patients is dehumanizing, the medical student may also imitate this pattern (Roter and Hall 1992).

I came to recognize the importance of a good bedside manner early in my medical training. However, it was during my residency training in dermatology at the Mayo Clinic when I finally mastered my technique. I learned my bedside manner by observing the excellent physicians who were my teachers. Each had his own style; some had a quiet, gentle approach while others were more forceful and commanding. But, they all showed warmth and concern for patients. Perhaps what made the greatest impression on me was that all patients were treated with equal dignity and respect. And bear in mind that we saw patients from all walks of life—some rich and famous to those with meager means. From this excellent exposure, I borrowed what I considered the best traits from each of these physicians and developed my own style of bedside manner that I would use for the rest of my career.

The influence of life experiences and books

Added to this learning process were my previous life experiences. I had wanted to be a doctor all of my life, and I very early sought ways to learn how to better interact with people. I sought out jobs as a camp counselor and hospital orderly. During my high school years I discovered a book in my father's library that changed my life. That book is Dale Carnegie's *How to Win Friends and Influence People.* In short, the book stresses developing your personality, showing an interest in others, being sympathetic and respectful and remembering the benefit of a smile. After reading the book and applying the recommendations, I went from an average, little-noticed student to vice president of my senior class and president of the Junior Red Cross. That book would play a definite role in my future success as a physician as would other books in the humanities.

As I grew more confident, I developed a better and more outgoing personality. I wanted to help people, and I was confident that nothing would prevent me from becoming a doctor. I would soon learn that it would take more than a friendly, personal style to be perceived as competent by my patients. It takes proficient medical skills as well as a better understanding of the patient's concerns to achieve that goal.

The importance of empathy

An integral part of a good bedside manner is empathy. Freud (1955) describes empathy as "a means by which we are enabled to take up any attitude at all toward another's mental health." To put it in the simplest terms, put yourself in somebody else's shoes. Empathy, compassion, and communication are really the essence of a good bedside manner. By listening to the patient and being empathetic, a doctor can not only gain the patient's trust but can also arrive at a diagnosis more quickly and accurately (Bellet 1991).

Conclusions

The best way to teach empathy and a good bedside manner is to have good medical teachers as role models. In addition, medical students would benefit to see firsthand what patients have to experience. A good example is an intensive program called "hospitalization week," an idea developed at the Ben-Gurion University Medical School in Israel (Carmel 1986). Medical students there are not only given courses in basic communication skills and medical ethics but some are also hospitalized, after which they discuss with their classmates their reactions to this experience. Furthermore, they take courses on families in crisis, conduct interviews with dying patients and their families, and observe patients in intensive care. The goal is to enhance empathetic feelings in these medical students and to help them develop a good bedside manner. This should be the goal of all medical schools in this country. We need to better prepare our doctors to deal with the emotional aspects of a patient's illness and to understand how they affect other family members.

*I have been surprised to note the
readiness with which high-grade young
men, graduates from medical institutions
which are models for our time, yield to
the temptation of machine-made diagnosis.*

William J. Mayo, M.D.

3

The Cardinal Rules of a Good Bedside Manner

One does not need specialized psychological training to learn and apply what I consider some of the most important rules of a good bedside manner. The seven principles I have chosen are straightforward and based on common sense.

- Put the patient at ease
- Be kind and courteous in your approach
- Convey a sense of confidence
- Make the patient and the problem important
- Be a good listener
- Answer the patient's questions and anticipate his or her concerns
- Be positive and reassuring whenever possible

Put the patient at ease

A smile after introducing yourself, a warm handshake, and a "How can I help you?" are often all that is necessary to put a patient at ease. When a warm greeting pleases the patient, the same warm behavior is often returned to the doctor (DiMatteo 1979; DiMatteo et al. 1986). "Sorry if I kept you waiting" goes a long way to reduce any tension resulting from the patient having to wait for what may at times seem like an eternity. Everyone hates to wait. For the patient, their time is just as important as the doctor's. Doctors should try to schedule their appointments so that patients seldom have to wait. Long periods of waiting lead to frustration among patients and sometimes to hostility toward the doctor and staff. Always inform patients of any delays and give them reasons for the wait. They should also be made to feel as comfortable as possible during the wait.

If patients seem deeply troubled, touching a hand or shoulder will help reassure them that you are sensitive to their emotional concerns. Sitting down with a patient, rather than standing, and maintaining eye contact reduce authoritarian posture and help convey a sense of individual attention. This approach also suggests, whether true or not, that you are not in a hurry. With today's concern over inappropriate sexual behavior, touching a patient—no matter how brief or confined to the hand or shoulder—can carry a risk with certain patients. But doctors should trust their instincts and not be afraid to exercise this touch that has for centuries been recognized as a component of compassionate patient care.

Talking with patients involves both verbal and nonverbal communication (Blondis 1982). Nonverbal communication, better known as body language, includes gestures like a smile, a frown, a warm handshake, and the way one stands when addressing another person. Body language is something we often use to help express our inner emotions. The patient's interpretation of these gestures can influence the doctor-patient relationship as much as spoken words. A frown, a look of disgust, or frequently looking at your watch are types of nonverbal communication that the patient may interpret as negative. On the other hand, a smile, paying close attention to the patient's words, maintaining good eye contact, and appearing genuine in the interview will usually be interpreted positively and will help put the patient at ease. Paying attention to the patient's nonverbal behavior is also important in assessing both the patient's physical and emotional state. The information given and received must be clear. If the verbal and nonverbal information provided by the patient seems incomplete, careful questioning can often fill in the gaps.

You may set the stage for a positive doctor-patient relationship well before your first encounter. The patient's choice of the doctor, when that is possible, may come from prior knowledge of your reputation and skill, especially from the reports of satisfied patients. In the American Medical Association's 1993 survey of patients on the subject of choosing a physician, respondents ranked the quality of care their highest priority, the cost and personal recommendations lowest. This, however, was not my experience. My patients who stated in their initial visit "you come highly recommended" or "you have a wonderful reputation" for the most part were immediately at ease. Perhaps their preconceived trust was the reason for their comfort.

A patient's first impression of a doctor can also be the result of conversation with a receptionist or other staff member. A friendly, well-informed, and professional support team, expressing an interest in helping the patient, is often the start of a good doctor-patient relationship. People at all levels of the health care team should convey warmth, sympathy, and understanding so that a patient feels important from the very beginning, not just a number or a collection of complaints. No one likes to be treated as a number.

A doctor's personal appearance may also influence a patient's first impression. Patients like their doctors to be well-groomed. In my interviews with patients, most prefer their doctors wear a white coat, perhaps because it conveys cleanliness: A white coat is also perceived as professional. Patients often "dress up" for their medical appointments, a sign of respect deserving reciprocity.

Be kind and courteous in your approach

People often come to doctors because they fear illness. Some worry that a doctor may misunderstand their concerns. A kind and courteous approach with an awareness of the patient's dignity and possible lack of any medical knowledge can help allay that fear and form the beginning of a strong doctor-patient bond. Conversations with patients should use terms the patient can understand, not medical jargon.

Address a patient properly by showing respect for age and gender. Addressing people by first name during the initial visit has become common, especially with the younger generation. I personally do not consider this proper or courteous, especially when addressing the elderly. When in doubt, use the patient's surname, preceded by Mr., Mrs., or Ms. or Miss (young adults and children are exceptions). This denotes respect and usually commands the same respect from patients. Of course, with time, a first-name relationship may result.

Being kind and courteous also involves an understanding of a patient's religious beliefs, differences in cultures, and how differences in gender prompt different responses.

Do not underestimate the strength patients derive from their religious beliefs (Pereira 1995). The use of prayers and religious articles should be encouraged and respected. The importance of prayer in the healing process has been the subject of recent studies at several medical centers (Marwick 1995). For those of religious faith who have observed the power of prayer, these studies may seem superfluous. Spiritual and religious practices foster a sense of well-being and can provide solace in a time of crisis (Grossman 1996).

Another important consideration is the care of patients from other cultures (Shuban 1980). This is especially important in large metropolitan areas where the population is typically diverse. Health care providers need to have some knowledge of how these cultures vary. For example, emotional pain in many cultures is translated to physical pain (Zborowski 1952; Zola 1966). This can complicate the physician's efforts to discern any real physical ailments. Asian cultures consider it a sign of weakness to display strong emotions among strangers. Health care workers need to determine how familiar a patient is with Western medicine and try to understand ethnic differences (Grossman 1996).

When patients cannot speak English, you may need to expand the history taking process to include family members (Blondis 1982). It will require all your communication skills. Listening carefully will convey an attitude of acceptance. If patients feel you do not understand or respect their beliefs, you may not be trusted. All efforts at communication will fail. By displaying an accepting attitude, you will allow patients a chance to find a safe and comfortable level where they will be more willing to share their feelings. It is especially important that non-Western patients be treated with warmth, patience, respect, understanding and dignity. Doctors should not necessarily discourage their use of native herbs and native healers, as they will often use them anyway together with Western medicine.

Gender differences also must be considered. Women have a tendency to ask more questions after a doctor's explanation (Wallen 1979). As a result, female patients often obtain more information than do men. Female patients are also more likely to admit to tension and ask for help than males (Stewart 1983). They also appear to have more positive experiences with their physicians than males (Hooper 1982) and they find it easier to disclose information about themselves (Aries 1987). It has been reported that women pay more attention to their health and are more compliant with their doctor's orders. Men tend to withhold their feelings and often pay less attention to their health needs. Sometimes doctors need the friendly help and influence of a spouse or partner to encourage a loved one to seek needed medical care. A doctor's kind and courteous approach to a recalcitrant male patient can often win over the man's confidence and instill a desire to seek help.

Convey a sense of confidence

Studies have shown that patients who like their doctors are often more compliant and have more confidence in their doctors' abilities (Lazarre 1975). A friendly, personal style does not necessarily translate into patient confidence, but it certainly helps (Buller and Buller, 1988). Other factors that may contribute to a patient's high confidence in a doctor are the physician's background, medical training, specialty board memberships, and reputation in the community.

The doctor should be expressive both in speech and manners. A non expressive demeanor on the part of the doctor may be interpreted as a lack of interest in the patient's problem. The doctor's air of self-confidence can contribute to the patient's recovery even at this early stage of the encounter (Kass December 1992).

Make the patient and the problem important

Patients like to feel that they and their problems are the most important of the doctor's day. To this effect, the doctor must give the patient undivided attention. Distracting phone calls and interruptions by staff members should be avoided unless absolutely necessary. Be sympathetic and interested even if the patient's complaint seems trivial. Taking notes during the interview will often show the patient that you consider what he or she has to say important.

Avoid appearing rushed, even on the busiest of days. A good bedside manner can often prove more important and satisfying to the patient than the amount of time allotted for the patient's visit. If more time is needed, arrange an early follow-up visit and encourage the patient to call if there are further questions. Be sure patients can reach you by phone through an answering service or by giving your home number in special cases. Phone calls from patients should be returned promptly. Sometimes, just the knowledge that the doctor can be reached is all the patient desires. In my experience, few patients abuse this service.

Be a good listener

"My doctor doesn't listen to me" is one of the most common complaints among patients. One study finds that doctors often interrupt the patients after only eighteen seconds into interviews (Beckman 1984). Patients are like open books. Gain their confidence and just listen. Some patients may feel threatened by the doctor's presence. This should not prevail if you first put the patients at ease. Encourage the patients to tell all they can about their problems. Then help guide them in the right direction as you begin to suspect the nature of their problem.

The art of interviewing a patient is knowing which questions to ask and how to listen to the answers. Taking notes adds to the patient's confidence in the ability of the doctor to listen. Physicians should never discuss their personal problems with their patients.

Answer the patient's questions and anticipate the patient's concerns

The patient comes to you for answers. Often you can make a diagnosis during the initial visit but may need additional visits, laboratory tests, or X-rays for confirmation. You should always keep in mind that the patient may be thinking the worst, fearing a serious disease like cancer. Often there will be enough information from your first examination (if thorough) to reassure the patient that the problem is not serious and that you do not suspect a life-threatening disease. Be careful to explain the use of words like "tumor," as many patients assume that all tumors are malignant.

If the diagnosis is clear, you may then discuss treatment options with the patient. If a surgical procedure is indicated, a more thorough explanation might require the knowledge of a qualified surgical specialist. If a biopsy is performed, the results should be conveyed to the patient as soon as possible. The results of laboratory tests and X-rays should be thoroughly discussed with the patient. If a result comes back that could prove serious, the patient should be contacted promptly for an early return visit.

When communication is good, the patient is more likely to understand the information you provide and is more likely to ask you to explain any information that is not clear (Emanuel and Dublar 1995).

Some doctors are reluctant to give a patient bad news. Sometimes doctors do this to ward off the sadness it creates inside (Quine 1983). One study also reported that a small percentage of patients feel they cannot cope with a frank discussion of their medical problems (Tuckett 1985). Sometimes this results from a lack of confidence in their doctors. Yet there are some patients who want to avoid information altogether. Doctors should respect this attitude but strive to gain the patient's confidence by giving the best care possible in the absence of adequate communication.

Be positive and reassuring whenever possible

After the initial examination of the patient, the doctor should communicate a clear understanding of the problem and a desire to help. Never, however, reveal a "suspect diagnosis" especially if what you suspect is serious. To give a serious diagnosis before it is accurately confirmed places a heavy and often unnecessary emotional burden on the patient. It can be brutal to give a patient a diagnosis of cancer that later proves to be incorrect. Saying you "don't know" but will do your best to find out will be well received by the patient. In most situations, building a good understanding of the patient and the problem often avoids the need for more complicated testing.

Perhaps the ability not only to acquire the confidence of the patient, but to deserve it, to see what the patient desires and needs, comes through the sixth sense we call intuition, which in turn comes from wide experience and deep sympathy for and devotion to the patient, giving to the possessor remarkable ability to achieve results.

William J. Mayo, M.D.

4

Bedside Manner and the Patient's Expectations

When it comes to health, connections exist between the mind and body that we still do not understand. Negative thoughts can bring negative results, even in the hands of the most skilled doctors. Accordingly, establishing a positive rapport with the patient is important and should be done at the earliest possible stage of the patient's care.

Too often I have heard people say they dislike a particular doctor. They may, however, have stayed with that doctor because of reputation, loyalty, or proximity to the patient's home or office. In almost all cases, I have found the dislike results from the fact that the doctor was not listening, had acted disinterested, or had not developed a bond with the patient so that there could be an exchange of ideas and emotions. In some cases, the patient was not allowed to participate in decisions regarding care. Other complaints were that the doctor seemed arrogant, blunt, or callous. Doctors should always be open and ready to review care plans with the patient and be willing to listen to the patient's desires. They should be ready to explain to the patient at intervals why a particular course of therapy needs to be continued or changed, especially if healing has been slow.

Emanuel and Dubler (1995) have suggested that the ideal physician-patient relationship can be summed by the "Six Cs." which are:

- Choice
- Competence
- Communication
- Compassion
- Continuity of care
- Conflict of interest (avoidance of)

Choice and continuity of care are especially important for patients with chronic conditions or cancer. By choosing and keeping the same doctor, patients can feel secure in the knowledge that the physician knows their history, has their records, and can therefore better anticipate their needs and fears. Patients who are forced to frequently change physicians, which may occur in some managed-care plans, will find it difficult to establish firm and understanding relationships with their doctors.

The placebo effect

Patients often have tremendous expectations of our health care system since we practice high-tech medicine. Unfortunately, we still do not know if all our therapies are truly effective or even necessary (Pickering 1979). It is very likely that a good bedside manner contributes greatly to the benefits seen from therapy prescribed. This could be due to the placebo effect. Placebo studies have shown that the idolization of the physician can have important therapeutic effects (Lasagna et al. 1954). I, for one, consider the placebo effect a benefit to patient care. The *placebo effect* occurs when a doctor prescribes a medication or a therapy that plays no direct physiological role in treating the patient's disease, yet the patient recovers often more quickly than expected. The placebo effect is enhanced by the patient's faith in the physician and a belief in the treatment prescribed. The mind heals the body.

HMOs and even some major medical centers are starting to include alternative forms of medicine like biofeedback, relaxation techniques, acupuncture, meditation, and yoga (Russell 1996; Podolsky 1996). HMOs that stress preventive health care as both good medicine and good economics are recognizing a lucrative opportunity in these alternative therapies in the public interest. Some insurance plans are considering covering herbal and homeopathic remedies. Skeptics point out that the benefit of these alternative techniques has to do with the patient's belief that they work, and demonstrate the placebo effect like that found in trials of new drugs. To illustrate their popularity, in 1990 it was estimated that Americans made 425 million visits to providers of unconventional therapy (Eisenberg et al. 1993).

Intuition

Another mind-body connection that deserves discussion is human *intuition*. Intuition is "knowledge based on insight or spiritual perception rather than on reasoning." Parents may have this insight when relating to their child's health. Parents may take their child to the doctor because they instinctively know the child is ill, even if the immediate outward signs of disease are not readily apparent. Doctors would be wise to pay some heed to these intuitive perceptions.

I am aware of several instances of intuition playing a role in the patient's ultimate diagnosis. One that stands out is the case of an intelligent, middle-aged woman who visited her doctor, convinced in her mind that she had breast cancer, even though she had felt no lumps in her breasts. On examination by her physician, no lumps were palpable. Her mammogram read normal, showing no evidence of breast cancer. The doctor correctly advised the patient to continue performing self-examinations and to return in one year unless a lump was found. Instead, because of her overwhelming concern, the woman returned in three months and insisted on a repeat mammogram. This time the mammogram revealed a small tumor which a biopsy proved cancerous. The patient underwent removal of the cancer and made a full recovery.

This case shows a rational, intelligent patient who had an intuitive insight about her body that she could not ignore. In her case, it may have proved life saving. Intuition, or a "gut feeling" of this type is rare, but it should not be dismissed. Perhaps some diseases could be diagnosed earlier if doctors would just listen to their patients' concerns and react positively to any intuitive feelings that seem reasonable.

The influence of age

The patient's expectations and the doctor's approach to bedside manner can be different depending on the age of the patient. As our population ages, chronic illness, most experts agree, will be the focus of future medicine. Developing a good doctor-patient relationship with the elderly is crucial (Kass 1992). Elderly patients, especially those beyond the age of 65, grew up in an age when doctors were more highly regarded than they are today. In the early part of the twentieth century, doctors were held in high esteem by society in general. To some, they were almost godlike because of their recognized long-term training and special skills. In small communities, the local doctor often lived in the largest house in town and was considered a pillar of the community. This doctor of the past who made house calls, delivered most of the babies, and was there when needed for care and advice remains vivid in the memories of many elderly people. This total commitment to patient care may be missing in today's medical profession (Greenberg 1990).

Elderly patients in my experience are often less demanding, feel more vulnerable, and are easier to win over if a proper bedside manner is practiced. Unless they have had a prior bad experience, they generally enter the physician's care with a more positive attitude, a cautious respect, and a sense of confidence. I especially enjoyed treating the elderly. They always seemed genuinely pleased with my care and could more easily express their praise. As they gained trust in me, they proved to be my most loyal patients and seldom left my care unless forced by geographic changes. Establishing a good bedside manner with the elderly requires respect, gentleness, a positive attitude, a little time to listen, and a sense of humor. The rewards as a doctor will be loyalty, trust, and often warm friendships that only enhance the joy of practice.

Elderly patients tend to have a different perception of the expected and proper role of the patient in our new health care setting. They are confused by the inability to stay with their own doctors as they transfer into managed-care plans. They are accustomed to medical care as it used to be. They don't understand why they can't see specialists whenever they wish. Governmental changes in Medicare are often not fully explained to or are poorly understood by the elderly. As our elderly population increases, doctors and other health professionals must be better prepared to help guide these older people through their so-called "golden years," which for many of the elderly is one of the biggest misnomers in the English language.

With advancing age, we still want to be loved. But for those of us with a chronic disabling disease, it becomes increasingly difficult to maintain a healthy self-image. We feel more and more isolated. For the elderly especially, love is what you do, not what you say.

The doctor-patient relationship for the pediatric patient is often more complex because it is a three-way relationship—the doctor, the child, and the parents (Schwartz 1995). The pediatric physician needs to establish a strong rapport with both the child and the parents. In fact, often the whole family needs to be considered when treating a child. With some modifications, the same cardinal rules of a good bedside manner apply to the pediatric patient. Until the child is old enough, the parents need to speak up for the child's health needs. As they grow older, children should be encouraged to talk directly with their doctors about their treatments and concerns.

The examination of the pediatric patient should be tailored to the age of the patient. Infants and small children are best left in a carryall or stroller, although some parents prefer to have their children on their lap. Older children often like to sit on the examination table and participate in the history taking. Teenagers may be interviewed with or without a parent, depending on the circumstances. Sometimes it is critical to get both the parents' and adolescent's views of the problem, as they may be quite different. Some doctors who treat children choose to do so without a white coat, thus relieving some of the child's anxiety. An alternative is to use a colored laboratory coat. In many instances, instructions and treatment plans should be written down for the parents and possibly for the child.

The hospitalized patient

For the hospitalized patient, a good bedside manner is critical. Perhaps this is how bedside manner got its name. These patients are often very ill, may be recovering from surgery, and may be scared and lonely. A good night's sleep can be difficult to achieve in a hospital. The illness, pain, a lack of restful sleep, and a possible encounter with a night nurse can all leave the patient in a bad mood before the doctor makes hospital rounds. For these hospitalized patients, the doctor's visit is the most important event of the day. If possible, the doctor should make it a positive one. The news you present will not always be good, but *how* you present that news is most important. You should be sympathetic and gentle and try to reassure the patient that you will do all you can to help. Husbands, wives, and parents of the patient should also be kept informed of progress and be part of the team, especially in major treatment decisions or when surgical procedures are to be performed.

A cheerful greeting, a holding of the patient's hand, and a sincere "How do you feel today?" may be all that is needed to lift the patient's spirits. Take time to listen to the patient. Try not to appear rushed. Sitting down on the edge of the bed or in an adjacent chair will help convey warmth and a sense of special attention and caring.

The patient and family will want to hear about the results of surgery, recent tests, what medications are being prescribed, and what side effects (if any) can be expected from therapy. The patients will also want your opinion of any progress. The sweetest words to the hospitalized patient next to "you are going home" are "you are doing well."

In my practice in a university medical center, I observed that my patients often seemed to recover faster and respond better to therapy if I was upbeat and full of encouragement. I regularly reassured them that I would work to ensure as rapid a recovery as possible. This proved to be an important morale-builder for my patients, especially when their responses to therapy seemed slow. The healing touch for hospitalized patients is, in my experience, absolutely essential to their welfare and can potentially shorten their hospital stays. Studies have shown that good doctor-patient communication is related to improved recovery from surgery, decreased use of pain medication, and shorter hospital stays (Mumford 1982).

For the seriously ill or dying patient, encouraging a "will to live" is often the most powerful medicine. For the dying patient, it may be the only "medicine" left to give.

Video education

Because of the increased demands on doctors and nurses in managed care, video-taped education programs for patients are being used more and more (Chase 1995). These programs are offered to help patients become better informed of and more comfortable with discussions of their health care. These videos, properly done, can remove physician bias and ensure that everybody gets the same information. Producers of these videos say they tend to enhance rather than take away from the doctor-patient relationship. After seeing a video, the patient should meet with the doctor to discuss any questions. The doctor and patient can then make decisions regarding the future course of therapy. As technology advances, these educational programs and the Internet will probably be even more widely used by patients.

At the close of a man's life, to estimate his worth it is wise to see him in relation to his life surroundings, to know not only the part he played as an individual, but also as a component part of the great events to which he contributed in the betterment of mankind.

William J. Mayo, M.D.

5

The Dying Patient

At no time are doctor-patient and doctor-family relationships more important than during end-of-life care. Unfortunately, doctors are not very good at handling the dying patient. What a dying patient wants in his or her last days is comfort and freedom from pain. Most dying patients also prefer to die at home. Yet, as a recent nation-wide study reports, few of the wishes of dying patients are honored (Support 1995). The study reveals that a majority of the doctors who cared for these patients never even looked at reports that included the patient's desires at the time of death. Often absent was any communication between the doctor and the patient's family. The sad result? Some patients who were kept alive were worse off than if they had been allowed to die. Some families lost all or most of their savings in this end-of-life struggle (Brink 1995).

Hospital care

Most Americans today still die in hospitals. Many lie alone in strange surroundings, attached to the multiple tubes and machines of our high-tech medicine. Although they receive quality care from skilled nurses and doctors, they are often kept alive because no one wants to make the decision to terminate life. In this controlled atmosphere these patients are often robbed of their dignity. Sometimes it is the patient's vital signs alone that are kept "alive" by doctors who refuse to give up hope and by families who can't let their loved one go despite the hopelessness of the situation.

The Support study (1995) further reveals that half of the patients who died had moderate to severe pain during their final three days of life. The medical team's assessment of a patient's pain was not routinely provided to the physician in charge. In nearly all of the cases, physicians misunderstood the patient's and family's preferences regarding use of heroic measures to keep the patient alive. Living wills, which are designed to protect a patient from heroic measures at the time of death, were simply disregarded.

My own experience with the death of my parents highlights these conflicts and the difficult decisions that many families have to make when a loved one is dying.

My mother, age seventy-five, was admitted to one of the world's most prestigious medical centers for emergency surgical treatment of bowel diverticulitis. To further complicate her health, she had been taking cortisone prior to this episode for a rare disease that progressively destroys the kidneys. As a result, her immune system was somewhat compromised. Following the initial surgery her large abdominal wound opened up. She returned to surgery, where a large mesh gauze was sewn over the abdominal wound. Because of her fragile condition, she was given only light anesthesia during the operation and suffered great pain. She told my oldest brother that the pain was so intense she had "been to hell and back." As her condition deteriorated, I hurried from California to try to be at her side before she died. I made it just in time. When she saw me, she smiled, squeezed my hand tightly, and didn't let go. She was unable to speak. That evening she went into a coma. My father remained at her side constantly. Soon my large family of five brothers and two sisters arrived.

My father was anxious to try to keep my mother alive, hoping for a miraculous recovery. Unfortunately, none of the doctors or nurses on my mother's medical team ever sat down and discussed with us the choices we needed to make and whether the situation was hopeless. They wanted to do more medical procedures to assess the status of her lungs, but I convinced my father that this would only cause her further pain and suffering. The doctors at one point also told us about a new, experimental antibiotic that might be helpful for the rare type of pneumonia my mother had developed. They told us the medication carried a high risk of liver damage, among other side effects. I spent the next two days trying to convince my father that the dangers of the drug would far outweigh its value and that we should avoid any further heroic procedures or medications. He finally agreed.

On life support, my mother's vital signs stayed normal. At this point, however, I was convinced that she would not survive. She stayed on life support for another two months because my father still had hope. I finally came up with a logical idea my father might agree to. I suggested that he ask the medical team to take my mother off all life support for a period of fifteen minutes. If she showed any signs of life, even the blink of an eye during the fifteen-minute period, the team would put her back on life support. He agreed. She showed no signs of life. Only then did my father accept that his wife of over fifty years had left for a better place.

I had watched my mother endure so much suffering and the indignity of two months on life support. Although the medical team was excellent, sympathetic, and caring, they could have helped my father consider terminating life support much earlier. They did not. My mother had no living will.

I have often wondered how many additional procedures would have been done and how long my mother would have remained on life support had I not been a physician with enough influence to prevent further intervention. Both my mother and father had to suffer needlessly far too long.

My father at age 86 was transferred from a nursing home in Florida to a local hospital, where he died after three days. He had led a very healthy and productive life until about three years prior to his death, when he developed progressive senility. He entered the hospital with severe congestive heart failure and pneumonia. His kidneys were no longer functioning. He had a living will clearly stating that when he was nearing death he wanted no heroic measures to keep him alive, only something for the pain to keep him comfortable. Even so, the doctors placed him on forced oxygen therapy as they started around-the-clock morphine. When it was obvious my father was at a terminal stage, my family asked his attending physician to take him off oxygen. Five hours off oxygen, he was gone. A few other family members and I were at his bedside at the time of his death, but none of his doctors were available to talk with us.

The Support study was an eight-year study of 9,105 patients from five teaching hospitals in the United States. The report concludes that doctors don't always listen to what patients want, are not always honest with bad news, and often manage pain poorly during end-of-life care (Lo 1995). This is a disturbing report. One of the problems we doctors face is that we hate to admit defeat, which we feel if a patient dies. When there is no longer any hope for a patient's survival, doctors must give up further attempts to save the dying patient. Doctors must not regard this decision as a sign of failure. As doctors we must allow patients to die, even though we must not intentionally kill (Kass March 1992).

Families of dying patients should also know that our high-tech medicine and methods themselves are not sound reasons for keeping the hopelessly ill patient alive. At a time when managed care is undermining our autonomy, we need to give our doctors better training in talking with patients about life-sustaining methods. We must teach them to do better relieving pain, to be more aware of patients' desires, and to do a better job helping patients and families make the difficult decisions at end of life (Lo 1995). Doctors are often unable to cope with the dying patient because they simply don't know how. Medical students, medical residents, and nurses need more training on how to discuss death and dying with elderly patients who are still vigorous. We need to focus on hope for a peaceful death rather than on prolonging life.

In his excellent book *How We Die* (1994), Sherwin Nuland writes:

> The greatest dignity to be found at death is the dignity of life that precedes it. It is the dignity that proceeds from a life well lived. The real event at the end of life is our death, not the attempts to prevent it.

He goes further to say that no woman or man should be left alone to die and that physicians should not abandon their patients at the time of death. There is a therapeutic value in a physician simply being there at the patient's death (Suchman 1988). People need a doctor's healing touch, even when healing is no longer possible. "When we mourn, it should be the loss of love that makes us grieve," writes Nulund, "not the guilt that we did something wrong."

Hospice care

To have more control over one's death, a patient needs to stay out of the hospital. People who die at home with loved ones around or in other supportive environments usually do better (Blondis 1982). This is where hospice service comes in. A *hospice* is a health care facility or a system of professional visits and supervision for the supportive care of the terminally ill. The Medicare/Medicaid hospice package includes nursing care, physical therapy, social workers, pastoral care, volunteers, and a medical director (Gurfolino 1994). A hospice program offers palliative care to any dying person who has opted not to have continuous, curative care. Its main goal is to enhance the quality of life remaining. Management of pain and the control of symptoms are the primary areas of hospice expertise.

Patients with Medicare or Medicaid who request hospice care must be referred to the service by a medical doctor who must judge that the patient has only six months or less to live. This can be difficult for the physician because dying from some diseases such as Alzheimer's is hard to predict. Hospice care addresses the physical, emotional, and spiritual needs of both the patient and the patient's loved ones and considers the wishes of both the patients and their families. To qualify, the patient must have a home and a family member or loved one at home for support. Volunteers are also important, as the caseload is heavy. Hospice care may also be financed by private insurance companies plans. The guidelines are similar to Medicare.

I made specific inquiries about the homeless people in San Francisco who obviously would not qualify for hospice care. When government funds or private funds are available, the homeless who are dying can sometimes be placed in residential hotels. Another option are the "Gift of Love" sites supported by Mother Theresa. Nurses in hospice care are usually on the front lines when it comes to caring for the poor and the homeless. They are concerned with the availability of medical services for all regardless of one's ability to pay (Hicks 1996).

More and more, patients want to die at home, so the demand for hospice care is growing. Full reimbursement for visiting nurses and other health care workers is often difficult to obtain. Private donations are often needed to help support hospice programs. For nurses, the same emotional rewards of home health care are achieved, but with a different emphasis. Hospice care is palliative care only. In the home, hospice patients are more content. The relief of pain and discomfort is often better achieved than in the hospital.

Today's care of the dying patient need not be depressing or unrewarding work. By applying a warm and compassionate touch, doctors and nurses can help patients feel better during the last days of their lives.

The trained nurse has given nursing the human, or shall we say, the divine touch, and made the hospital desirable for patients with serious ailments regardless of their home advantages.

Charles H. Mayo, M.D.

6

The Changing Role of Nurses Under Managed Care

Nurses have been held in high esteem since the days of Florence Nightingale, regarded as the founder of modern nursing. Throughout the years, there have been many changes in the nursing profession. Not so long ago, nurses could be easily identified by their starched white uniforms, white shoes, and distinctive caps. With time more men have entered the nursing profession. Perhaps as a result, the dress code for nurses has been relaxed. A nurse today may be seen wearing athletic shoes and carrying a stethoscope (Stephany 1992). Nonetheless, nurses remain a symbol of hope and compassion for the sick and wounded. Their care is best exemplified by words like dedication, devotion, and self-lessness.

Expectations of patients

Nurses, like doctors, need to establish strong bonds with their patients. Failure to do so can be a major source of frustration and even anger among patients who expect the nurse to be there to care for them (Strauss 1995). Nurses must have adequate time to spend with patients to provide those special comforts unique to nursing. The hospital nurses I have interviewed uniformly tell me their major concern is the serious lack of time, a "time crunch" that has only become worse with the introduction of managed care.

The public in general is not always aware of the complexity of nursing. Many of a nurse's activities are hidden or taken for granted. They are often noticed only when they are not delivered (Wolf 1994). For the sick and disabled, the presence of a nurse alone is reassuring, especially in a hospital or home care setting (Brown 1986). There still remains a lack of appreciation, and few clinical studies directly support the positive contribution good bedside nursing makes to the overall welfare of the patient. History and general observations tell us the benefits are considerable.

With the introduction of managed care, hospitals have come under attack as they face new financial pressures. Today the public's primary criticism of hospitals is that they are inefficient, impersonal, and place too much emphasis on achieving financial success (Aiken 1994). The more like a business a hospital becomes, the lower the level of public confidence and trust. Unfortunately, nurses often bear the brunt of these complaints (Gordon 1996). As hospitals are faced with cost-cutting demands, especially in states where participation in managed care is high, nurses are being replaced by untrained technicians (Shindul-Rothschild 1996). Patients complain that they are not getting quality care. Registered nurses (RNs) are placed in administrative roles and are not available to provide the hands-on care so essential to the patient's healing process (Gordon 1996). Hospitals need to strive for a better balance between the business side of their operations and needs of patient care provided by doctors and nurses.

The nursing shortage

There is a growing concern about the vacancy rate of nurses in our nation's hospitals (Aiken 1994). More than 75 percent of hospitals report nursing shortages. Enrollment in nursing schools has fallen 26 percent since 1983, sounding an alarm as to the future supply of RNs. Why the current shortage of nurses? Many nurses are leaving the profession. The demand for nurses in hospitals is rising as the nursing care needs for the average patient is reportedly growing. Hospital intensive care units have increased in number. Finally, many nurses have been replaced by Licensed Practical Nurses (LPNs) and aides (Aiken 1994).

More unlicensed assistant personnel (UAPs) have also entered the scene. These UAPs generally have six weeks or less of formal training, usually in a community college, after which they enter the hospital workforce. Because they are less costly to hire than RNs or LPNs, they are popular with many managed-care plans. Unfortunately, this is all happening at a time when most hospitalized patients are just too sick to have their care delegated to semi-skilled health care providers (Aiken 1994).

UAPs have taken over many of the patient care tasks previously performed by RNs. These tasks are often important in establishing the nurse-patient relationship. For example, the ritual of the patient's bath allows the nurse to check the patient's skin and become aware of any physical or emotional abnormalities not previously recognized. Most importantly, it is a time when the nurse gets to know the patient and can explore the patient's inner thoughts (Wolf 1994; Strauss 1985). Most patients who enter a hospital have no idea what to expect. They are often as worried about their jobs and the welfare of their families as they are about their illnesses (Blondis 1982). This is where the RN and a social worker can work together to help patients gain a clearer picture of what to expect upon leaving the hospital. "Communication should facilitate recognition of the link between a patient's mental state and the physical influence of illness" (Roter 1992). Failure to bring out the patient's hidden tensions and emotions because of a lack of good bedside manner can lead to a poorer recovery and, in some instances, a crippling psychological disability, as sometimes occurs in men after a heart attack (Mumford 1982). Proper counseling in the hospital can often give the patient peace of mind, trust, and a sense of well-being better than any medication that could be prescribed (Peabody 1927).

Home health care

As the pressures of hospital nursing increase, more and more RNs are turning to home health care nursing. Nurses are also doing more outside the hospital, serving as counselors or educators in doctors' offices and governmental agencies and as private entrepreneurs. In managed-care plans, nurses do more teaching and may hold classes on subjects such as AIDS prevention, prenatal care, and family planning. Managed care is looking closely at home health care as it becomes a popular trend with nurses (Dee-Kelly 1994). As patients must be discharged earlier and earlier from the hospital, they often return home less able to care for themselves and need continuing medical supervision.

The demand for long-term home care is also increasing as our population grows older; at the same time, we see a corresponding increase in the prevalence of chronic diseases and disabilities. The increased life expectancy is expected to double the number of people 65 years and older by the year 2002 to 45 million. The number of people aged 84 and over will grow 200 percent in the same period (Rice 1983). The demand will increase the number of aged and disabled persons who prefer to have their medical services provided in their homes rather than in nursing homes or other institutional settings (Harrington 1994). Under the right circumstances, older people seem to do better at home and are a lot happier. The question is, with the increase in the number of older citizens, will the demand for home health care eventually outstrip our available medical resources?

Most of the nurses I have interviewed tell me how much they enjoy home health care nursing. Why? They have more control of their time and can work directly with the patient. By going to the patient's home, nurses are able to get a better sense of the patient's financial and domestic situation and can observe the patient surrounded by family and friends. This helps give the nurse a chance to provide a healing touch and to establish a warm relationship with the patient based on trust. Successful home care depends on trust (Doherty 1994). Unlike working in a hospital, 90 percent of a nurse's duties are supportive and psychological, and only 10 percent procedural and administrative in home health care.

Yet to be established is how well home care nursing is working. Many questions must be answered. Who should get home care? How much should they get? What does home care accomplish? Who should pay for it? At present, commercial insurance companies and managed-care companies have offered only minimal home care benefits (Humphrey 1988). Politics will undoubtedly play a major role in future decisions concerning home health care and how it fits into our rapidly changing health care scheme.

Role of the nurse-practitioner

Managed-care will probably heighten the role of nurse-practitioners and clinical nurse specialists, whose higher levels of training qualify them to provide some of the services performed by physicians. Specialization of nurses has been one of the most important changes in nursing in the last few decades. The function of these nurses is no longer much different from that of physicians. As more of these specially trained nurses move into independent practice, they are welcomed by managed-care because they are considered by some to be more cost-effective than doctors. Knowing this, these nurses may take on an even more prominent position in the practice of medicine in the years ahead.

Even today, in some areas of the country, patients are no longer able to see a physician in- itially. Instead, they are assigned by a doctor's office or a managed-care administrator to the care of a nurse-practitioner unless the patient's condition is too serious or complex for the nurse to handle. How well this will be universally re- ceived by a population used to making its own choices and wanting the care of a personal physi- cian is yet to be determined. Will it break the bond of trust already established by the patient's physician, so essential to the patient's welfare?

Nurse-practitioners now deliver babies, prescribe medications, provide support and ad- vice to patients, and act as database managers. Nurse-practitioners already play a prominent role in many HMOs and do an excellent job pro- viding health care services previously done solely by physicians. They can successfully form nurse-practitioner/patient relationships and pro- vide quality care. Nurse-practitioners point to studies showing they can handle 60 percent to 80 percent of the tasks a primary care physician can perform and without consultation (*American Jour- nal of Nursing*, 1993). Physicians remain skeptical and defensive about such reports, but by recog- nizing their capabilities, these nursing specialists have become more widely accepted by physicians. However, it will take time for the majority of physicians and the public to fully accept this newer approach to health care. Managed care, politicians, and governmental agencies could eventually make this a pivotal issue because of the potential cost savings.

Medicine gives only to those who give,
but her reward for those who serve is
'finer than much fine gold.'

Charles H. Mayo, M.D.

7

The Good, the Bad, and the Ugly: Real-Life Experiences

The following story was written by a parent who had mostly positive experiences with the doctors who cared for his son. Yet he writes as if his own experience is so unique that he wants to appeal to all doctors to deliver the important elements of a good doctor-parent relationship. This father reminds us how important it is to have a doctor who answers our questions and is patient with us in our desire to understand (Emanuel and Dubler 1995). The story comes from the April 5, 1993 edition of *American Medical News*. It was written by James N. Fancher, an *AMN* contributor and computer consultant, about his son and his experiences with doctors since his son's illness.

Case #1

Doctor, don't think I am placing myself above you—I admire anyone who can stick to it long enough to come out a winner as you have done. But if you haven't been on the other end of the stethoscope or syringe, please listen.

My family and I have spent more than 180 days in various hospitals over the last few years. Many of these experiences have been positive, thanks to the compassionate professionals involved in our care.

I'd like to describe a few of these in the hope that you can learn from these good examples.

One of our son's hospitalizations required that he be there three or four days while tests were run. Our gastrointestinal specialist made rounds each day and explained the upcoming battery of tests. She always answered my questions, even when I asked the same one two or three times, and her answers were always straightforward.

At the end of the fourth day, the physician walked in with a folder of test results, pulled a chair up by the bed and said those words a family member hates to hear from a doctor's mouth: "I don't know."

I wasn't angry. It is critical for you to understand that "I don't know" is an acceptable answer. It doesn't mean you've failed. This would be the case if you hadn't exercised all the tools at your disposal to seek an answer or if you had been too proud to ask for help, or if you hadn't been open and honest with the patient and family.

On a business trip, I took my son with me. In a motel on the way home, he woke up critically ill. I had a list of his doctors' home phone numbers and I called them at 1:30 A.M. to explain the situation. They called ahead to the emergency room at the nearest hospital to arrange care for my son until he could be safely transported home. The telephone access I had to my son's physicians made all the difference to us. Do your patients have your home phone number?

Accessibility and access are the key. Don't take yourselves so seriously that you can't touch your patients and your patients can't touch you. And, Doctor, if parents tell you something is wrong with the child on the exam table and you ask why we think so, please don't close your mind when we say, "I'm not sure, but something is just not right." This kind of parental thinking, while irrational, illogical, unjustifiable, and unscientific, is rarely wrong. Furthermore, Doctor, don't treat me as an adversary. If you take the time to talk to me, you will discover how important I am to the care of your patient. Treat me as a member of the

*team. If you treat me as an outsider, I will give
you nothing but agony, since you are dealing
with the dearest thing in my life, a member of my
family.*

The ability to reach a doctor any time, day
or night—that is the kind of accessibility patients
want from their physicians, although few doctors
today would agree to give out their home phone
numbers. This father also touches on intuition
and how important it is for doctors to recognize
this phenomenon, especially when parents some-
how know their child is ill (see chapter 4). Finally, the writer points out the importance of
having both a parent or guardian being a part of
the team in the care of a child or other family
member and a doctor who understands the importance of good communication (Herman 1985).

The following stories come from my personal interviews with families.

Case #2

*Several years ago, my mother was diag-
nosed with abdominal cancer. She was referred
by our family doctor to a surgeon for an ex-
ploratory surgical procedure. We were unable
to talk to the surgeon prior to the surgery.*

*My husband, four other family members,
and I gathered in a rather drab waiting area in
the hospital while the surgery was being performed. We were anxious to learn if the cancer*

had spread or if it could still be removed. We still had hope.

After about one hour, the surgeon entered the waiting area and his immediate words were: "No sense sitting around looking gloomy. The cancer has spread. I did all I could do, so there is no reason for you to hang around. You might as well go home." And he left.

We were devastated by this doctor's cold, callous approach, which left us dazed and further depressed. We all knew in the back of our minds that the news would not be good, but what we needed from the surgeon was just some kindness, warmth, and consideration for our grief. My mother was a wonderful person and she deserved to be treated with dignity. I truly believe that the surgeon didn't even know my mother's name. I am convinced that to him she was just a body with a disease. It is hard for me to even tell this story, and when I do, I still cry. It was such an ugly, painful experience that could have been so different had the surgeon shown just one ounce of compassion.

This is a sad story of an ugly experience that could have been prevented. The surgeon should have been aware that every grieving family in this situation needs a doctor's sympathy, compassion and support (Suchman 1988). One gets the impression that this doctor discovered the patient's problem was hopeless, considered the patient's life over, and thought the family needed to go forward. However, the doctor also may have experienced feelings of failure. As a result he was unable to face either this family's grief or his own (Quine 1983). Some physicians do feel inadequately prepared to approach terminally ill patients and their families (Carmel 1986). We need to better train our physicians to handle these emotionally charged situations.

Case #3

I was undergoing chemotherapy following the removal of breast cancer. It meant going every other week to a treatment area in our local hospital for intravenous (IV) medication, which often resulted in nausea, extreme fatigue, and discomfort. The cancer specialist in charge saw me briefly to put in the IV. The nurse looked in on me from time to time to see if the IV was running well. Otherwise I was alone. This was an especially depressing and fearful time for me, and I am sure it showed on my face. One day during this treatment, my wonderful family doctor came by, took one look at me, and gave me a big hug. He said, "I could see you needed that." He was so right. His brief hug so warmed my spirits and renewed my hopes. I will never forget that hug for as long as I live.

How important it is for doctors to be aware of their patient's emotions and to take a few moments to apply a healing touch in times of special need. This is an example of "a medicine of friends" (Siegler 1993).

Case # 4

About five years ago, I began having unusual symptoms in my legs. Because my symptoms persisted, I started to worry that there could be something seriously wrong with me. I saw two general medical doctors, who both dismissed my symptoms as due to stress. At times I wondered if I were just being a hypochondriac, but my worry only increased. I decided to see a well-respected neurologist in my town and called his office for an appointment. His receptionist said he was so busy that he could not see me for six weeks.

I began to cry on the phone. With this, the receptionist said she would leave a message with the doctor to call me back. One hour later the doctor returned my call, listened to my symptoms, and said he would see me early the next day. At 7:30 the next morning, this doctor spent twenty minutes asking me questions about my problem. After a thorough physical, exam we went back to his office. He explained that my symptoms were due to a bulging disc in my back. He suggested I start some special

back exercises and see him again in three
months. Just knowing what I had brought me
tremendous emotional relief. I was glad to know
the symptoms weren't "just in my head."

I sent the doctor a basket of blooming tulips
and a card telling him how appreciative I was of
his time and concern. He sent me a card telling
me that he planted the tulips in his backyard so
that he could enjoy them longer. This doctor
retired last year. I know many of his patients
will miss him because he had a reputation of
being a truly caring doctor from the "old
school" of medicine. He was a compassionate
doctor with a great bedside manner that was
truly healing.

Case # 5

My family and I are members of a well-es-
tablished health maintenance organization. Re-
cently, I noticed a growth on my arm and made
an appointment to see one of my medical plan's
dermatologists. He was able to see me after a one-
week wait. When he entered the exami-na-
tion room, he took a quick look at the
growth, didn't say a word, and handed me a
sheet of paper that he asked me to read. While
I was reading, he said "the growth is nothing,"
he had seen it many times before. He looked at his
watch after being in the room for what seemed like
no more than a minute and proceeded to leave.

I said, "Wait. Would you please explain this better for me?" Although the paper he handed me said dermatofibroma on it, he then said that it was probably an ingrown hair. I said, "No, it can't be an ingrown hair so please remove the growth." He then said, "Go home. If you start to have anxiety about the lesion come back and I will remove it." He also said that the removal would leave an unsightly scar. The obvious impression I got was that he wanted to dismiss me as quickly as possible. I told him I already had a lot of anxiety about the growth and my choice was for him to remove it. He then proceeded to numb the lesion with an injection of an anesthetic and punched the lesion out with a large round punch.

Unfortunately my two little girls were in the room with me. Because of the way the doctor treated me, they started to cry. Even the nurse in the room seemed nervous because the doctor was in such a hurry. There was a lot of tension in the room. When my girls and I got to my car, we all cried. I felt like I had been abused and insulted. This doctor showed no compassion. He gave me the feeling that my complaint was too trivial. Needless to say, I will never see that doctor again.

Here's what I mean by "hurry-up" medicine. This doctor immediately conveyed to the patient that her problem was trivial and that handing her a printed handout was a satisfactory substitute for listening and communication. Physicians who take the time to communicate are often considered more competent by patients (Bernstein 1987). This is also an example of how medical care can be delivered in a cold, disinterested way that quickly destroys a patient's confidence (Buller 1988). The patient was thinking the worst and had to demand the treatment she desired.

Case # 6

I belong to an HMO, one of two plans offered by my employer. The other is a private insurance plan that is just too expensive for me and my family. I was assigned to a general medical doctor in the HMO. Over the years I saw him on a few occasions for minor problems like colds and the flu. He always seemed in a hurry, my visits were short, and at times he seemed somewhat arrogant.

About two years ago, I noticed some rectal bleeding, and my bowel movements seemed irregular. I saw my doctor at the HMO when the signs did not subside after two weeks. He listened to my story for about ten minutes, quickly examined my rectal area, and said, "You have some hemorrhoids that account for your bleeding. Stop worrying." He gave me a prescription for a rectal suppository and dismissed me. I saw him on two further visits, as the problem con-

tinued. Each time the doctor told me "not to worry." During the last visit, I cautiously asked him if I could get another opinion. He became furious with me, insisting he had a lot of experience with conditions like mine and a second opinion was not necessary. That night my husband told me we needed to go outside our plan and seek another opinion, even if we could hardly afford it.

Since we lived in a university town, I was able to get an appointment with a gastroenterologist at the medical school. He did a barium Xray of my bowel, put a tube into my colon, and took a biopsy. He said the biopsy results would be ready in a few days and would be sent to my HMO doctor. I made an appointment for the next week. I felt scared and uneasy about seeing my doctor after I had, without his knowledge, gone to another doctor. When I entered his office, he did not look at me or greet me but simply asked me to sit down next to his desk. His next words were, "Well, you have cancer of the bowel." He pulled out an Xray to show me. No one except someone with this same experience can know how you feel when you are told you have cancer. It is like an immediate death sentence. Without showing any emotion the doctor said, "You need to make an appointment with one of our surgeons." But I couldn't move. I seemed frozen to my chair. "Oh, all right," he said, "I'll call for you." There was never at any time consideration from this doctor for how I might be feeling about this frightening diagnosis.

The surgeon I saw was wonderful. She had a cheerful smile and was gentle, kind, and compassionate in dealing with my fears. She always seemed so confident, which also gave me confidence in her. The morning of the surgery she came by to see me, told me she would do her very best for me, and gave my hand a tight squeeze. At that moment my fear of the surgery left me. I knew that I was in good hands and that my prayers for recovery would be answered. Fortunately, the cancer had not spread. The surgeon was confident they got it all out. I am, so far, doing well. I do not want to return to this other doctor in whom I had lost all trust, faith, and respect. Because of my diagnosis, I have to stay with my HMO, as I am no longer considered "an acceptable risk" should I leave the plan.

This is how a doctor can let ego get in the way of good judgment. It nearly cost this patient her life. It further emphasizes that patients sometimes need to challenge their doctors. When in doubt, patients should demand a second opinion (Rubin 1993). How this doctor presented himself on the patient's return visit from the university specialist is a clear example of how devastating negative nonverbal communication can be for patients (Blondis 1982). The doctor's total lack of compassion and empathy and the way he told the patient she had cancer was brutal.

Under the care of the surgeon, things changed for the better. The surgeon's compassion and self-confidence helped contribute to the patients well-being and possibly to her recovery (Kass December 1992). This patient's experience exemplifies both the best and the worst that can occur in doctor-patient relationships. In the end, this case becomes an example of how the healing touch is essential to the patient's comfort and the healing process (Kass 1992; Siegler 1993)

It is a poor government that does not realize that the prolonged life, health and happiness of its people are its greatest asset.

Charles H. Mayo, M.D.

8

Other Consequences of Managed Care

The United States today spends more on health care than any other country in the world. As a result, American society has concluded that doctors are a major cause of increasing health care costs and that they need to be managed and controlled. Since the early 1980s, economic and decision-making power has been shifting from doctors, hospitals, patients, and families to insurance companies and governmental agencies (Siegler 1993).

Employers, insurance companies and the government declared rising health care costs a crisis in this country and looked to managed-care as a solution. Unfortunately, they did not consider that managed-care with its practice guidelines might have a negative impact on the doctor-patient relationship. For these new plans and reimbursement systems to be effective, they would have to limit the time doctors could spend with their patients, limiting communication and the time to establish rapport. In addition, third-party payers would now be involved in deciding which therapies are beneficial and which ones are not.

Diminishing quality of health care

Medicine today no longer rewards doctors for time-consuming interviews. As a result, the time necessary to develop a rapport with patients as well as the time to make careful clinical observations can be seriously impaired (Lazarus 1994). Primary care doctors are feeling overwhelmed as they are asked to manage medical conditions that were once clearly not in their purview. Resentment is growing among subspecialists. Strong financial pressures exist to keep down referrals and shorten hospital stays. Academic medical centers are finding it hard to compete in the managed care marketplace as they are too expensive. Yet academic centers are where our new ideas and technological innovations come from (Lazarus 1994).

Distrust and tension has increased among doctors and patients in some managed-care settings (Larsen 1996). The doctor-patient interaction relies on trust and confidence to develop into a stable relationship. Seigler (1993) writes that the relationship between doctor and patient should be a "medicine of friends," not a "medicine of strangers." Doctors who develop relationships like friendships with patients will develop trust rather than control. In a "medicine of strangers," trust is replaced by guidelines, rules, and control. "Friendship works both ways and enriches both patient and doctor. It makes a successful outcome more pleasing, and it alone has the power to redeem tragedy" (Bascom 1993).

Doctors and patients should see themselves not as adversaries, but as allies. In fact, establishing a good doctor-patient relationship is not only good medicine but also perhaps the only option under bureaucratic control that cannot be totally regulated in a managed-care setting. It is the one area that doctor and patient can maintain autonomy and try to cling to those values we have recognized as beneficial to health care in the past. But to maintain this important component of patient care in the face of cost-cutting reform, doctors will have to disregard those forces that tend to erode this important relationship. Patients may have to demand it be preserved for the benefit of all.

Profitability alone should not be allowed to dictate health policy decisions in this country. Physicians are ethically bound by the Hippocratic oath to act independently in the interest of their patients (Wasnick 1996). Health care management should also be guided by ethical standards that maintain our recognized virtues in medical practice. They should not interfere with the doctor-patient relationship but instead should encourage it for the mutual benefit of their doctors and patient members. As I have stressed, a good doctor-patient relationship can play an important role in the reduction of health care costs.

New technological advances, efforts toward cost containment, governmental intervention, changes in medical care delivery, and rising public demand are some of the factors that are causing "personalized medicine" to seem increasingly obsolete. The key to keeping the healing touch alive is to convince doctors, patients, medical educators, managed-care plans, insurance companies, and governmental agencies of its profound importance in the practice of medicine.

Diminishing morale among health care professionals

What newly trained doctors meet as they enter the managed-care arena may prove surprising and distressing. Doctors generally like to be independent. In medical school they are trained to be free thinkers. In managed-care plans, things are often predetermined. The major source of unhappiness today is the collision of medicine with health care management and profits.

A recent survey of young California doctors has uncovered a surprising degree of unhappiness among physicians fresh out of medical school (Greenberg 1995). Much of their unease comes from the growing concern of finances entering the day-to-day practice of medicine. Fewer than 10 percent of these young doctors have had generally good experiences with corporate health care plans. Only 21 percent say cost has never affected their medical decisions. Finally, 31.4 percent surveyed said they would not have become doctors if they had it to do over again.

The only encouraging part of the report is that the vast majority have nevertheless been happy with their physician-patient relationships, even though two-thirds say they have been dissatisfied with the amount of time they can spend with patients. It is shocking to hear that so many doctors are so disgruntled so soon in their careers. Unless society puts pressure on these managed-care groups to allow physicians more freedom, I fear the quality and quantity of medical school applicants will diminish as new applicants become aware of these problems. Although these survey results may be unique to California, where there is a surplus of physicians, they suggest a worrisome trend nationwide as managed-care plans proliferate.

Declining salaries

In this country physicians' salaries are slowly declining (Mitka 1996; Simon 1996). With fewer monetary incentives and less ability to expand their practices and income, some doctors are beginning to lose their enthusiasm for their chosen profession. Those able to leave medicine are doing so, while others are pursuing further education in other fields like business administration. Based on anecdotal information and discussions with my colleagues, it appears some are looking for other careers that can provide more secure monetary and psychological rewards. Clearly, physicians' goals and attitudes must adapt to our changing health care system if the joys and rewards of medical practice are to be retained. It has been and always should be a privilege to be a doctor. Physicians should never lose sight of why they entered medicine: to help and heal the sick. To paraphrase a San Francisco physician who so poignantly wrote to me regarding a mutual former patient:

> Since I started my practice in 1980, everything is now different, but what has not changed is the delight in caring for others and facing the challenge of illness.

What is encouraging, however, is the rising number of medical applicants. An *AMA News* report from December 1993 finds a record 42,808 students applied that year to the 126 U. S. medical schools, of which 16,307 applicants were chosen. Of those accepted, 42 percent were women. This application ratio is a striking increase above the low application rate of 26,721 in 1988. At Harvard in 1994, medicine was that year's most popular career choice among seniors, ahead of business or academia, the usual forerunners. Apparently, what older doctors envision as tumultuous times ahead, young doctors see as an opportunity (Anders 1994). Medical educators report that medical students are looking for intellectual satisfaction as well as financial security (Mechanic 1978).

Increased stress levels

Those of us who become doctors understand early on we'll have our share of stress to deal with. Doctors undergo long, arduous training with many examinations to pass before becoming qualified to practice medicine. During this training, they see patients in all stage of physical and emotional disrepair, including those seeking treatment as a result of increased social problems such as drugs or violence.

If this were not enough stress, along comes the health care revolution, driven primarily by cost. The new medical ethic is to try to prevent disease and treat illness with the most cost effective methods available. Accordingly, physicians are often under pressure to see patients rapidly and to enhance the care plan's financial productivity.

Clearly, one of the main sources of angst for physicians today is the pressure for profits. And as a result, according to R.M. Tenery, (Tenery 1996) doctors have lost a "shared vision," the perception of our profession being based on the qualities we try to emulate from observing good doctors of our day. Today, many physicians do the best they can while seeing the most patients possible with as little cost possible to the medical plan.

Consequently, patient trust erodes. How can doctors respond to their patient's wishes when limitations are imposed from an outside source? Our commonalty as physicians is fragmenting and our goals are becoming diverse.

Increasing potential for litigation

Physicians who provide good information are often considered by patients to be more competent and caring and are less likely to be sued (Bernstein 1987). Patients often have unrealistic expectations of physicians and medical science and believe that when something bad occurs, someone has done something wrong. Patients want both caring and treatment. When doctors forget about caring, patients often become frustrated and angry even when they are cured. Patients are especially disturbed when their medical care is delivered in a cold, disinterested way. Good communication and caring can help prevent lawsuits even when the physician is clearly at fault. Studies show that education of patients reduces the frequency of litigation (Shapiro et al. 1989). Good communication and positive feelings between doctor and patient are interpreted as caring and concern and will elicit a positive response. The physician will be viewed as having acted in good faith.

Studies also reveal that "defensive medicine" does not so much prevent medical malpractice lawsuits as help physicians win them, should they occur. Defensive medicine includes ordering extra medical procedures and tests, getting additional consultation, and extensive documentation.

A need for legislation

I fear patients will suffer needlessly from "hurry-up" medicine. I am convinced some diseases will be missed or improperly treated unless doctors are allowed to spend adequate time with patients, are given the freedom to refer patients to appropriate specialists, and are able to prescribe and treat patients as they deem necessary.

A recent Medical Board of California Action Report states:

We are concerned that the business model of managed-care, as implemented by some plans, may inappropriately restrict the physician's ability to practice quality medicine and may thus have negative consequences for the consumer (Shumacker 1997).

Lawmakers in Washington, D.C. are also beginning to address this issue with proposed tough new legislative reforms for managed-care companies. It is my hope that books like this one will help stir up reforms to improve our present managed-care system and encourage egalitarian exchange, empathy, compassion, and communication—all essential to providing high-quality medical care.

The practice of medicine is a person-to-person profession. It cannot be replaced by robots or computers. Nor can it be supplanted completely by printed handouts or video programs for patients (Chase 1996). Doctors and their patients must communicate directly with each other, even when handouts or video programs are used.

I'm reminded of the ancient medical proverb: *Cure sometimes, relieve often, and comfort always.* Doctors today can still only cure sometimes. They can often relieve pain and suffering. But due to restrictions on their time and other constraints on their practice under managedcare, they are less and less able to offer the comforts so important to the healing process. Medicine in America today is often able to cure but is often unable to care (Harrington; Cassel 1996).

Doctors have an enormous responsibility to help heal the sick. They have many wonderful procedures and medicines at their disposal to help alleviate suffering. But at the heart of all this lies the doctor-patient relationship, the bedside manner, the healing touch. This must remain the cornerstone of medical education and good patient care today. Perhaps Dr. Leon R. Kass presented the case most succinctly in his John and Roma Rouse Lecture at the Mayo Clinic in December 1992:

> Thanks to medicine's great technical prowess, doctors (and patients) sometimes forget that the physician both serves and cooperates with immanent powers of self-healing and self-maintenance working within, power in the absence of which medicine would be impotent.

Finally, I am fervent in my belief that talented, highly-trained doctors should cling to the preservation of the healing touch despite the pressures of today's medical climate. We knew when we first started training it would not be easy to be a doctor and now we face changes in the system that are likely to be here to stay. We must unite in our efforts to make it a better system for our patients and our profession. We must be active participants in the debate and in the planning and implementation of health care in this country (Nadelson 1996). As physicians, we are committed to taking care of people, and I hope we can always find satisfaction in being able to make the world a better place for those we help and heal.

Bibliography

Aiken, L.H. "The Hospital Nursing Shortage: A Paradox of Increasing Supply and Increasing Vacancy Rates." *In Health Policy and Nursing: Crisis and Reform in the U.S. Health Care Delivery System,* Edited by C. Harrington, and C.L. Estes, 300-312. Boston: Jones and Bartlett, 1994.

Anders, G. "Changes in Medicine Widen the Usual Gap among Physicians." *Wall Street Journal,* 20 June 1994, 1(A) and 5(A).

Aries, E. "Gender and Communication." Edited by P. Shaver and C. Hendrich. *In Review of Personality and Social Psychology. Vol. 7.,* Newbury Park, Calif.: Sage Publications, 1987.

Bascom, G.S. *Sketches from a Surgeon's Notebook in Empathy and the Practice of Medicine.* Edited by H.M. Spiro, M.G.M. Curnen, E. Peschel, and D. St. James, 31. New Haven and London, England.: Yale University Press, 1993.

Beckman, H.B., R.M. Frankel, and J. Damley. "The Effect of Physician Behavior on the Collection of Data." *Annals of Internal Medicine* 101 (1984): 692-696.

Bellet, P. and M.J. Maloney. "The Importance of Empathy as an Interviewing Skill in Medicine." *Journal of the American Medical Association* 266 (1991): 1,831-1,832.

Bernstein, A.H. *Avoiding Medical Malpractice.* Chicago: Pluribus Press, 1987.

Blondis, M.N. and B.E. Jackson. *Nonverbal Communication with Patients: Back to the Human Touch.* New York: J. Whiley and Sons, 1982.

Brink, S. "The American Way of Dying." *U.S. News and World Report,* (December 1995): 70-75.

Brown, L. "The Experience of Care: Patient Perspectives." *Topics in Clinical Nursing* 8, no. 2 (1986): 56-62.

Buller, M.K. and D.B. Buller. "Physicians' Communication: Style and Patient Satisfaction." *Journal of Health and Social Behavior* 28 (1988): 375-388.

Carmel, S. and J. Bernstein. "Identifying with the Patient: An Intense Program for Medical Students." *Medical Education* 20 (1986): 432-436.

Carnegie, D. *How to Win Friends and Influence People.* New York: Simon and Schuster, 1936.

Chase, M. "Videotapes Educate People about Disease, Minus Bedside Manner." *Wall Street Journal,* 30 October 1995, 1(B).

Dee-Kelly, P.A., S. Heller and M. Sibley. "Managed Care: An Opportunity for Home Care Agencies." *Nursing Clinics of North America* 29, no. 3 (September 1994): 471-481.

DiMatteo, M.R. "Nonverbal Skills and the Physician-Patient Relationship." *In Skill in Nonverbal Communication: Individual Differences,* Edited by R. Rosenthal. Cambridge, Mass.: Qelgeschlager, Gunn, and Hain, 1979.

DiMatteo, M.R., R.D. Hayes, and L.M. Primen. "Relationship of Physician: Nonverbal Conversation Skill to Patient Satisfaction, Appointment Noncompliance, and Physicians' Workload." *Health Psychology* 5 (1986):581-594.

"Doctors' Public Image Steady of Late, but Has Slipped over Time." *American Medical News,* Vol. 36 no. 17 May 1993): 9.

Doherty, M. S.J. Hurley, and C.B. Perfetti. "Suburban Home Care, Cost, Financing, and Delivery." *Nursing Clinics of North America* 29, no. 3 (September 1994): 483-493.

Eisenberg, D.M. et al. "Unconventional Medicine in the United States: Prevalence, Costs, and Patterns of Use." *New England Journal of Medicine* 328 (1993): 246-252.

Eisenberg, J.M. "Sociological Influences on Decision Making by Clinicians." *Annals of Internal Medicine* 90 (1979): 957-964.

Emanuel, E.J. and N.N. Dubler. "Preserving the Physician-Patient Relationship in the Era of Managed Care." *Journal of the American Medical Association,* Vol. 273, no. 4 (January 1995): 323-329.

Fine, V.K. and M.E. Therrien. "Empathy in the Doctor-Patient Relationship: Skill Training for Medical Students." *Journal of Medical Education* 52 (1977): 152-157.

Francher, J.N. "Do You Listen to Your Patients or Their Parents?" *American Medical News* 5 April 1993, 23.

Freud, S. "Group Psychology and the Analysis of the Ego." *In The Standard Edition of the Complete Works of Sigmund Freud.* vol. 18. Edited and translated by J. Strachey, 110. London: Hogarth Press, 1955.

Gordon, S. and C.M. Fagin. "Preserving the Moral High Ground." *American Journal of Nursing* 96, no. 3 (March 1996): 31-32.

Greenberg, B.K. "Whither Great Expectations: Bridging the Reality Gap." *California Physician,* Vol. 12 (December 1995): 29-31.

Greenberg, M.A. *Off the Pedestal: Transforming the Business of Medicine.* Houston: Breakthrough Publishing, 1990.

Grossman, D. "Cultural Dimensions in Home Health Nursing." *American Journal of Nursing* 96, no. 7 (July 1996): 33-36.

Gurfolino, V. and L. Dermas. "Hospice Nursing: The Concept of Palliative Care." *Nursing Clinics of North America* 29 no. 3 (September 1994): 533-546.

Harrington, C. "Quality Access and Costs." *In Health Policy and Nursing* Edited by C. Harrington and C.L. Estes. Boston: Jones and Bartlett, 1994.

Harrington, C. et al. "A Natural Long-Term Care Program for the United States: A Caring Vision." *Health Policy and Nursing,* Edited by C. Harrington and C.L. Estes, Boston: Jones and Bartlett, 1996: 490.

Helfer, R.E. "An Objective Comparison of the Pediatric Interviewing Skills of Freshman and Senior Medical Students." *Pediatrics* 45 (1970): 623-627.

Herman, J.M. "The Use of Patients' Preferences in Family Practice." *Journal of Family Practice* 20 (1985): 153-156.

Hicks, L. and K.E. Boles. "Why Health Economics in Health Policy in Nursing: Crisis and Reform." *In Health Policy and Nursing,* Edited by C. Harrington and C.L. Estes, 11-12. Boston: Jones and Bartlett, 1996.

Hilman, A.L., et al. "How Do Financial Incentives Affect Physicians Clinical Decisions and the Financial Performance of Health Maintenance Organizations?" *New England Journal of Medicine* 321 (1989): 86-92.

Hooper, E.M., L.M. Comstock, J.N. Goodwin, and J.S. Goodwin. "Patient Characteristics That Influence Physician Behavior." *Medical Care* 20 (1982): 630-638.

Humphrey, C.J. "The Home as a Setting for Care." *Nursing Clinics of North America* 23, no. 2 (1988).

Ingelhart, J.K. "The Struggle Between Managed Care and Fee-for-Service Practice." *New England Journal of Medicine* 331 (1994): 63-67.

Kaplan, S.H., S. Greenfield, and J.E. Ware Jr. "Assessing the Effects of Physician-Patient Interaction on the Outcomes of Chronic Disease." *Medical Care* 27 (1989): 5100-5127.

Kass, L. "I Will Give No Deadly Drug. Why Doctors Must Not Kill." *American College of Surgeons Bulletin* 77, no. 3 (March 1992): 6-17.

Kass, L. "The Doctor-Patient Relationship: What Does It Mean?" Presented as the John and Roma Rouse Lecture for Human Values in Medicine at the Mayo Clinic, Rochester, Minn., 16 December 1992.

Larson, E. "The Soul of an HMO." *Time,* 22 January 1996, 44-52.

Lasagna, L. et al. "A Study of the Placebo Response." *American Journal of Medicine* 37 (1954): 770-779.

Lazarre, R. et al. "The Customer Approach to Patienthood: Attending to Patient Requests in a Walk-In Clinic." *Archives of General Psychiatry* 32 (1975): 553-558.

Lazarus, G.S. "Managed Care in California." *Archives of Dermatology* 130 (1994): 1,534-1,542.

Lester, G.W. and S.G. Smith. "Listening and Talking to Patients: A Remedy for Malpractice Suits?" *The Western Journal of Medicine* 158 no. 3 (1993): 268-272.

Lo, B. "Improving Care Near the End of Life: Why Is It So Hard?" *Journal of the American Medical Association* 274, no. 20 (November 1995): 1,634-1,636.

Marwick, C. "Should Physicians Prescribe Prayer for Health? Spiritual Aspects of Well-Being Considered." *Journal of the American Medical Association,* Vol. 273, no. 20 (1995): 1,561-1,562.

Mechanic, D. *Medical Sociology.* 2d ed. New York: The Free Press, 1978.

"Medical School Applications Up" *American Medical News,* 6 December 1993, 26.

Mitka, M. "Doctors Pay Shrinks for the First Time in '94." *American Medical News* 39 (1996): 1, 9-10.

Mumford, E. and H.J. Schlesinger. "The Effects of Psychological Intervention on Recovery from Surgery and Heart Attacks." *American Journal of Public Health* 72 (1982): 141-151.

Nadelson, C.C. "Ethics and Empathy in a Changing Health Care System." *The Pharos*, Vol. 59, no. 4 (Fall 1996): 29-32.

Nuland, S.B. *How We Die.* New York: Knopf, 1994.

"Nurse-Practitioners Emerge as Key Players in the Debate Over Reform; MDs Will Fight Inroads." *American Journal of Nursing* (July 1993): 69-73.

Peabody, F.W. "The Care of the Patient." *Journal of The American Medical Association* 252: 813-818.

Pereira, T. "The Healing Power of Prayer Is Tested by Science." *Wall Street Journal,* 20 December 1995, 1(B), 4(B).

Pickering, G. "Therapeutics: Art or Science?" *Journal of the American Medical Association* 242 (1979): 649-653.

Platt, F.W. *Conversation Repair: Case Studies in Doctor-Patient Communication.* Boston, New York, Toronto, and London: Little, Brown, and Company, 1995.

Platt, F.W. and V.F. Keller. "Empathetic Communication: A Teachable and Learnable Skill." *Journal of General Internal Medicine* 9 (1994): 222-226.

Podolsky, D. "A New Age of Healing Hands." *U.S. News and World Report,* 5 February 1996: 71-74.

Quine, L. and J. Pahl. "First Diagnosis of Severe Mental Handicap: Characteristics of Unsatisfactory Events between Doctors and Patients." *Social Science and Medicine* 22 (1983): 53-62.

Rice, D.P. and J.J. Feldman. "Living Longer in the United States: Demographic Changes and Health Care Needs of the Elderly." *Milbank Memorial Fund* 61 (Summer 1983): 362-396.

Roter, D.L., M. Lipkin Jr., and A. Korsjurd. "Sex Differences in Patients and Physician Communication during Primary Care Medical Visits." *Medical Care* 29 (1991): 1,083-1,093.

Roter, D.L. and J.A. Hall. *Doctors Talking with Patients-Patients Talking with Doctors*. Westport, Conn. and London: Auburn House 1992.

Rubin, R. "When and How To Challenge Your Doctor." *U.S. News and World Report,* 10 May 1993, 63-66.

Russell, S. "HMOs Try Dose of Alternative Medicine." *San Francisco Chronicle,* 22 January 1996, 1(A), (4)A.

Schwartz, M.A. *Listen to Me, Doctor.* Aspen, Colo.: Mac Murray and Beck, 1995: 139-142.

Seigler, M. "Falling Off the Pedestal: What Is Happening to the Traditional Doctor-Patient Relationship." *Mayo Clinic Proceedings* 68 (1993): 461-467.

Shapiro, R.S. et al. "A Survey of Sued and Non-Sued Physicians and Suing Patients." *Archives of Internal Medicine* 145 (1989): 2,190-2,196.

Shubin, S. "Nursing Patients from Different Cultures." *Nursing* 80 (June 1980): 80.

Shumacker, A.E. "Board Member Speaks at Department of Corporations Hearing on Effect of HMOs." *Action Report, Medical Board of California* 61 (April 1997): 3.

Shindul-Rothschild, J. "Patient Care: How Good Is It Where You Are?" *American Journal of Nursing* 96, no. 3, (March 1996): 22-24.

Simms, C. "How to Unmask the Angry Patient." *American Journal of Nursing* Vol. 95 (April 1995): 37-40.

Simon, C.J. and P.H. Born. "Physicians' Earnings in a Changing Managed-Care Environment." *Health Affairs* 15, no. 3, (Fall 1996): 124-133.

Speedling, E.J. and R.N. Rose. "Building an Effective Doctor-Patient Relationship: From Patient Satisfaction to Patient Participation." *Social Science and Medicine* 21, (1985): 115-120.

Stephany, T. "As I See It." *American Nurse* 24, no. 5, (1992): 11.

Stewart, M. "Patient Characteristics Which Are Related to the Doctor-Patient Interaction." *Family Practice* no. 1, (1983): 30-35.

Stewart, M. "What Is A Successful Doctor-Patient Interview?" *Social Science and Medicine*, Vol. 19, no. 19 (1984): 167-175.

Strauss, S. et al. *Social Organization of Medical Work.* Chicago: University of Chicago Press, 1985.

Suchman, A.L. and D. A. Matthews. "What Makes The Doctor-Patient Relationship Therapeutic?" *Annals of Internal Medicine* 108 (1988): 125-139.

Support. "Principal Investigators for the Support Project. A Control Trial to Improve Care for Seriously Ill, Hospitalized Patients. The Study to Understand Prognosis and Preferences for Outcomes and Risks of Treatments." *Journal of the American Medical Association* 247 (1995): 1,591-1,598.

114   *The Healing Touch*

Tenery, R.M. "Have Physicians Lost Something Along the Way?
American Medical News, Vol. 39 (November 1996): 22.

Tuckett, D. et al. *Meetings Between Experts.* New York: Tavistock Publications, 1985.

Wallen, J., H. Waitzkin, and J.D. Stoekle. "Physician Stereotypes about Female Health and Illness." *Women and Health* 4 (1979): 135-146.

Wasnick, J.D. "The Physician's Ethic and Managed-Care: Reformation Parallels." *Pharos* 59, no. 1, (1996): 27-28.

Wolf, Z.R. "Uncovering the Hidden Work of Nursing." *Health Policy and Nursing,* edited by C. Harrington and C.L. Estes, 331-332. Boston: Jones and Bartlett, 1994.

Zborowski, M. "Cultural Components in Response to Pain." *Journal of Social Issues* 4 (1952): 16-30.

Zola, I.K. "Culture and Symptoms: An Analysis of Patients Presenting Complaints." *American Sociological Review* 31 (1966): 615-630.

About The Author

Dr. David Cram received his medical degree from University of Wisconsin Medical School, Madison, and trained for his dermatology specialty at the Mayo Clinic, Rochester, Minn. There, he earned a Master of Science in dermatology.

Upon completion of his medical training, he was assigned to the United States Air Force Base Hospital in Lakenheath, England, where he became Chief of the Department of Medicine. During that time, he received the Air Force Commendation Medal and rose to the rank of Lt. Colonel.

In 1971, Dr. Cram joined the staff of the University of California, San Francisco, where he became Chief of the Dermatology Clinic, and served as a teacher, lecturer and researcher.

After fifteen years in academia, Dr. Cram began a private practice in dermatology which he maintained until 1991, when he was forced to retire because of progressive Parkinson's Disease.

Dr. Cram is the author of dozens of scientific publications; among his numerous honors and awards, he is credited with starting the first Psoriasis Day Care Treatment Center in the country and was appointed Clinical Professor Emeritus by the University of California in 1991.

Addicus Books

Visit the Addicus Books Web Site
http://members.aol.com/addicusbks

Please send:

_____ copies of _____
                              (*Title of book*)

          at $_____ each   TOTAL   _____

          Nebr. residents add 5% sales tax   _____

          Shipping/Handling
             $3.00 for first book.
             $1.00 for each additional book.   _____

          TOTAL ENCLOSED   _____

Name _____
Address _____
City_____ State ____ Zip_____

          ☐ Visa ☐ Master Card ☐ Am. Express

Credit card number_____
Expiration date _____

Order by credit card, personal check or money order.
Send to:

                    Addicus Books
                    Mail Order Dept.
                    P.O. Box 45327
                    Omaha, NE 68145
          Or, order **TOLL FREE: 800-352-2873**